THE RADICAL REMNANT

BY
MIKE KEYES, SR.

WORD & SPIRIT
PUBLISHING

The Radical Remnant
Copyright © 2021 by Mike Keyes, Sr.
ISBN: 978-1-949106-60-2

Published by Word and Spirit Publishing
P.O. Box 701403
Tulsa, Oklahoma 74170
wordandspiritpublishing.com

*And on behalf of me, in order that there might be given me utterance in the opening of my mouth, **in every fearless, confident freedom of speaking,** to make known the mystery of the good news on behalf of which I am an ambassador in a chain, **in order that in it I may speak with every fearless and confident freedom as it is necessary** in the nature of the case for me to speak.*

—EPHESIANS 6:19-20 WET

*Ask on my behalf, that words may be given to me, so that, **outspoken and fearless,** I may make known the truths (hitherto kept secret) of the Good news.*

—EPHESIANS 6:19 WNT

*Like adamant stone, harder than flint, I have made your forehead; **do not be afraid of them,** nor be dismayed at their looks, though they are a rebellious house.*

—EZEKIEL 3:9

You see, says the Spirit of God, I am looking for just a select few. I don't need everyone. I just need the dedicated ones, because I can make up the slack and I can take up where others refuse to pick up their mantle. I can make up for the lost time of those who are choosing to be mediocre, and for those who are choosing to wallow with their flesh and lag behind. I can make up the difference. All I need are a few, and I am asking you to choose this night to serve Me with all of your heart and all of your soul and all of your mind and all of your strength.

I don't need everyone. I only need a few, and I am asking you to choose you this night whom you shall serve. Me? The world? Or your flesh? You choose.

Word of prophecy given by Apostle Mike Keyes, Sr., during church services at New Life Christian Church, Yelm, Washington, 1996.

CONTENTS

PART ONE

THE SITUATION

CHAPTER ONE

The Watchman's Responsibility

*I have set watchmen on your walls, O Jerusalem; they shall never hold their peace day or night. You who make mention of the Lord, **do not keep silent**.*

—Isaiah 62:6

*Son of man, **I have made you a watchman** for the house of Israel; therefore hear a word from My mouth, **and give them warning from Me**.*

—Ezekiel 3:17

According to 2 Timothy 3:1, we should know that we are living in perilous times. Now more than ever, it's vital we understand our role in the earth as ambassadors of Christ

(2 Corinthians 5:20). As official representatives of heaven, we are responsible for discharging our duties in the name of Jesus. One of those duties is that of a watchman. This is primarily what we are here for—to watch and then to warn. This is not just an Old Testament command. The Apostle Paul specifically identified this as a New Testament responsibility as well: *"Him we preach, **warning every man** and teaching every man in all wisdom, that we may present every man perfect in Christ Jesus"* (Colossians 1:28).

From the creation of Adam until the day Jesus returns, God has set His children in the earth as watchmen. We are responsible to preach, teach, and warn the world of what is happening now, what is coming soon, and what's at stake for each man's eternal destiny. In these perilous times, the devil is hard at work using his puppets in the secular arena to suppress the Body of Christ and silence our witness to the world. Of course, he has always been doing this, but now with the availability of social media, international discourse, technology, and the internet as it is in 2021 and beyond, he has tools to use to their full advantage that give him unprecedented access.

There is no shortage of gutless politicians, radical terrorists, anarchists, biased "news" personnel, social media censors, academic liars, false religious zealots, and Hollywood hypocrites who hate God, hate Jesus, hate Christians and the church, hate Israel, and hate anybody who disagrees with their revolutionary agenda to destroy America as we know it. They are no longer attempting to hide their hatred either. As former President Obama publicly stated, they want to fundamentally change America. They intend to replace capitalism with socialism and communism. They intend to wipe out the freedoms we've enjoyed for over two centuries. Specifically, for us, they intend to destroy our ability to fulfill the Great Commission of Mark 16:15-18. They believe they are on a march that cannot be stopped.

This is why the Body of Christ—the church of the Lord Jesus Christ—needs to exert itself now as *the army of the Lord*. And when I'm talking about the army of the Lord, I'm not talking about the vast majority of people who claim to be Christian and who are not, or may indeed be saved but are of none effect for the kingdom of God. I'm also not talking about the multitudes of so-called pastors who are nothing more than ignorant, deceived idiots at best, and dedicated wolves in sheep's clothing at worst. No sir! I'm talking about those of us within the army of the Lord who understand that there is an army within the army. They understand the times in which we live. They know the vital role they must play in these last days. They possess the courage and boldness to stand along the walls of the world, and boldly proclaim the truth without fear. They know they are God's watchmen who have a solemn duty to fearlessly warn people— wherever, whenever, and whosoever.

CHAPTER TWO

We Do Because
We Know

*And **do this, knowing the time, that now it
is high time to awake out of sleep;** for now
our salvation is nearer than when we first
believed. The night is far spent, the day is
at hand. Therefore let us cast off the works
of darkness, and let us put on the armor of
light. Let us walk properly, as in the day, not
in revelry and drunkenness, not in lewdness
and lust, not in strife and envy. But put on
the Lord Jesus Christ, and make no provision for the flesh, to fulfill its lusts.*

—ROMANS 13:11-14

We're told to do something because
we know something. If we know we
are living in perilous times, and if we know
the return of Jesus is as close as it is, we are

5

responsible to wake up and stay alert, because the night is far spent and the day is at hand. If it was far-spent 2,000-plus years ago when these verses were written, how much more are the times far-spent now?

Knowing this drives us to a place whereby we make the adjustments necessary to keep our swords as sharp as they can possibly be. We become compelled to make changes so we stay on that wall of warning like we're supposed to. We keep preaching the truth without apology or hesitation, as a watchman for God must. Romans 13:12 includes the word "therefore." In other words, because we know the times we're in, and we know we have responsibilities as God-appointed watchmen, we do what must be done to stay razor-sharp for Jesus. We cast off the works of darkness, put on the armor of light, and walk properly in the day in which we live. We cease the revelry (a casual, nonchalant, cavalier, party-type attitude about life), drunkenness, lewdness, lust, strife, and envy. We shut down the flesh completely, and refuse to allow it to have any avenue of expression in our lives. Like Paul told the Corinthians, we, like he, die daily (1 Corinthians 15:31). We get rid of all of that, and put on Jesus. That means we become mirrored reflections of Who Jesus is now, but also as important, Who Jesus was when He walked on this earth.

> *Do not be deceived: "Evil company corrupts good habits."* **Awake to righteousness,** *and do not sin; for some do not have the knowledge of God. I speak this to your shame.*
>
> — 1 CORINTHIANS 15:33-34

Paul was ashamed of how these Corinthian brethren were living. As I look around at the army of the Lord that I've seen in my ministry travels, I'm ashamed of many of them as well. I'm sorry to say the majority of them are disqualified for the work of God in these last days. There are a few here and there that God can use, but not many. *This must change.* Now, it's high time to awaken out of sleep. Not someday soon. Not a few years from now. Not when these lukewarm Christians get around to it. *Now!* That's my mandate from God. I am compelled to stir the pot. I'm compelled to challenge the soldiers in God's army to awaken out of spiritual sleep.

7

I know I can't get everyone on board, but I can get some, and I'm dedicated to do my part to find them and get them turned around for Jesus while we still have time to work. Remember what Jesus said: *"I must work the works of Him who sent Me while it is day; the night is coming when no one can work"* (John 9:4).

CHAPTER THREE

Be like Jesus

*Now when they saw the boldness of Peter
and John, and perceived that they were uneducated and untrained men, they marveled.
**And they realized that they had been with
Jesus.** And seeing the man who had been
healed standing with them, they could say
nothing against it.*

—ACTS 4:13-14

This is such a marvelous passage! If you
read Acts chapters 3 and 4, you'll see that
because of the mighty miracle wrought for the
crippled man who was laid daily at the Beautiful
Gate, Peter and John were arrested and brought
before the Sanhedrin to answer the charge of
unlawful outreach and evangelism. The enemies
of the gospel asked them one question: "By what

power or by what name have you done this?" (Acts 4:7).

Filled with the Holy Spirit, Peter boldly responded and laid out the case that all of us need to state before the world today whenever they try to shut us down. Here it is: *Jesus is the only way to salvation. There is no other name under heaven given among men by which we must be saved* (Acts 4:12). Period. Jesus said He is the way, the truth, and the life, *nobody comes to God except through Him* (John 14:6). He is not *a way,* He is *the way* to eternal life. That's it. There was none of what we see so often today—evasive waffling and wavering by so-called Christians, doing all they can to avoid declaring the simple truth that this is.

If somebody doesn't like that or disagrees with that, too bad for them. That's their funeral, not ours. I respond to people like that straight up. *Okay—you want to go to hell? Fine—go to hell!* When ministers and rank-and-file believers are bluntly asked if Jesus is the only way to salvation, they need to be the watchmen they're called by God to be. Answer just like Jesus did all throughout His public, earthly ministry.

Answer the way these early believers did. Tell it like it is, and let the chips fall where they may. And if we're threatened with reprisal, retribution, persecution of all sorts, or even death itself, we hold our ground and stand fast for the truth without apology. That's what these ungodly temple officials saw when they interrogated Peter and John, and what the world needs to see and hear from us today. Never forget this truth: *not every Christian who has been saved by Jesus has been with Jesus.*

Where is this kind of boldness in the secular world in which we live? This passage tells us that when they saw the *boldness* of Peter and John, and perceived that they were *uneducated and untrained,* they marveled in stunned astonishment. Not only were they shocked that such inferior individuals, in their opinion, could be used by God to bring about such a miracle, they took note that they had been with Jesus. How did they come to that conclusion? Because they looked like, talked like, and acted just like Jesus. Because of their in-your-face boldness, and because the miracle-man was standing next to them. That's how. The result? *They could do nothing against it!* That's where we need to be today with our outreach and evangelism. They were the living fulfillment of what Jesus said we should be and do:

> *Philip said to Him, "Lord, show us the Father, and it is sufficient for us." Jesus said to him, "Have I been with you so long, and yet you have not known Me, Philip? He who has seen Me has seen the Father, so how can you say, 'Show us the Father'? "Most assuredly, I say to you, he who believes in Me, **the works that I do he will do also; and greater works than these he will do,** because I go to My Father."*

> —JOHN 14:8-9, 12

Watchmen are supposed to watch as mirrored reflections of who Jesus was and what Jesus did. Nothing less. We're not left on earth by God to build some carnal kingdom for ourselves. We don't have to go off to some Bible school somewhere to be God's true watchmen either. Part of the shock these temple officials experienced was in part because Peter and John weren't "educated" or "trained," whatever that meant to them. They were just simple disciples of Jesus. Nothing more. But because they were saved and Spirit-filled, they were transformed from being a bunch of confused, fearful bags of useless verbal garbage, to front-line fighters in the army of the Lord! I love it! This is what we must become as members of God's army within the army. He doesn't need everyone who is a child of God. *He just needs the Radical Remnant.*

CHAPTER FOUR

What New Doctrine Is This?

*Then they were all amazed, so that they questioned among themselves, saying, "What is this? **What new doctrine is this?** For with authority He commands even the unclean spirits, and they obey Him." And immediately His fame spread throughout all the region around Galilee.*

— MARK 1:27-28

Continuing with what we brought out in chapter three, I want you to go back and look at how Jesus stirred the crowds with His style of ministry. Everywhere He went, demons feared Him and people talked about Him. He commanded respect from the demons He confronted, and also from the people who witnessed His ministry in person. When He

15

walked into a synagogue, people took a step back. When He was finished with ministry, people just stood there in awe and wonder.

Get out your concordance, and run the word "marveled" through the four gospels, and see how Jesus affected everyone as God's Watchman. His very presence commanded respect from the everyday Jew, from His religious enemies, from the Romans (Matthew 27:14/Mark 15:39), and especially from demons. When He confronted the madman of Gadara, the demonic tormentors were pleading with Jesus not to torment them! (Mark 5:7) Another example of this is how the temple guards reacted when they were told to go arrest Jesus.

> The Pharisees heard the crowd murmuring these things concerning Him, and the Pharisees and the chief priests sent officers to take Him. Then the officers came to the chief priests and Pharisees, who said to them, "Why have you not brought Him?" The officers answered, **"No man ever spoke like this Man!"**
>
> —JOHN 7:32,45-46

When the temple officers came to take Jesus, not only did they not interrupt His teachings and forcibly take Him away, they ended up standing there listening. They were spellbound. When the Pharisees and chief priests demanded to know why they hadn't brought Him by force, they replied to say they had never heard anyone speak like Jesus was speaking. In short, they probably said in reply: *Not only did we not arrest Him, but we got on His mailing list! We're monthly partners now, and we bought all of His books and flash drives at His resource table!*

Many will say, "Well, that was Jesus! I'm not like that!" Oh yeah? *Well, get like that—now!* Quit being part of a misfit collection of melba toast, milk-sop, triple-minded, zwieback, Krispy-Kreme, cotton-candy, cookie-cutter, cupcake, camouflaged, caramelized, cream-puff, clueless, confused, compromised, carnal Christians. We've got plenty of them all around us, and I hope to God you're not one of them! They're in pulpits and churches every Sunday all over the world. They're useless bodies in pews, disqualified to be used of God as watchmen because of the weak, spineless, gutless lives they live.

No, my friend. Jesus said the works He did we can do (John 14:12). Either we can say and do exactly that, or Jesus is a liar—and we know that isn't the case. The way our Lord lived as God's Watchman is the way we must live today. No more delays. No more excuses.

CHAPTER FIVE

The Man among Men

> *"So I sought for **a man among them** who would make a wall, and stand in the gap before Me on behalf of the land, that I should not destroy it, but I found no one. Therefore, I have poured out My indignation on them; I have consumed them with the fire of My wrath; and I have recompensed their deeds on their own heads," says the Lord.*
>
> —EZEKIEL 22:30-31

To avert divine judgment thousands of years ago, God was looking for a man among His people to stand in the gap and make a wall through intercession. This is where America is right now. As a country, we've flaunted our carnality in the face of a Holy, Righteous God long enough. We are now facing His anger, indignation, and judgment, and we'll end up exactly like Israel if we don't repent.

Think about that for a moment. God only needed *one man* among so many to take his place on the front lines to avert disaster. Unfortunately, He didn't find even one. Thankfully for us today, the situation is much better! There are millions of people praying for our nation, more than ever. Never in my lifetime have I seen such a surge in spiritual intercession and political activism from the Body of Christ as I see today. And specifically, many ministries and ministers have arisen solely for the purpose of shaking and waking an apathetic, lethargic, lazy, and anemic church. Remember, it doesn't take every Christian to make the wall and stand in the gap. It only takes a Remnant—the Radical Remnant.

My question to you is this: In God's eyes, are you a man or woman among them? Are you a cut above the rank-and-file Christian? Are you actively, passionately, and enthusiastically standing in the gap to make the wall that averts God's judgment upon America? Only you can answer for yourself. I've made my choice.

Several years ago, I met with many of my leaders in the Philippines, shortly before the 2016 USA presidential election. I told them then what I'm telling you today. Unless God steps in because we Christians woke up, repented, and stood in the gap like 2 Chronicles 7:14 says, the time will come when preaching the uncompromised Word of God will be labeled as *hate speech* and a *hate crime*. The convicted Christians will then be punished in all kinds of ways, such as loss of employment, loss of business profitability through boycotts or permits being refused or rescinded, being harassed at work or at school by teachers and classmates, and on and on we could go. Basically, it will be persecution by the ungodly at every turn, including but not limited to arrest, conviction, imprisonment, and even martyrdom. We're at that moment now. And if you don't think any of this can happen in America, you need to get your ignorant head out of the sand! It's already happening—and will continue to get worse unless God finds the kind of men among us to do what must be done to stop it.

> *For the eyes of the Lord run to and fro throughout the whole earth, to show Himself strong on behalf of those whose heart is loyal to Him.*
>
> —2 CHRONICLES 16:9

Just like in the Old Testament, God now searches back and forth (to and fro) across the world, looking for a particular kind of Christian to show Himself strong to. He's looking for the true watchmen—those who refuse to come down off that witness-wall and buckle under the demonically-inspired social pressure to compromise the message of salvation.

The reason God has to search for His watchmen is because they aren't readily found. They are the *Congregation of the Mighty* (Psalms 82), which is a much smaller army within the army. They are men among mere men—soldiers among mere soldiers. They are the Radical Remnant, who refuse to be commonplace. They have elevated their walk with God to a level that qualifies them to be used as conduits for God's power, anointing, protection, provision, and favor. When God locates these saints, He faithfully provides whatever they need to get the job done, and they feed on His faithfulness (Psalms 37:3). Jesus said we are here to shine gospel light on the darkness of a world without God, and most of them don't like it when we do (John 3:19-20).

Are you a man among men—a member of God's end-time special forces? A member in good standing within the Congregation of the Mighty? Or, are you just another body in a church chair on Sunday morning, useless to God and disqualified for every good work (Titus 1:16)?

In the Old Testament, Caleb was one of the two spies that gave the people a good report of faith. God said His servant Caleb had a *different spirit* in him (Numbers 14:24), and followed Him *fully*. These are the end-times watchmen God searches for throughout the whole earth. I could write an entire book on this man alone, he inspires me so much! In the Hebrew language, his name means *raging canine madness*. In other words, mad dog, or rabid dog! He was a bold and blunt servant of God who didn't care if you loved him or hated him. If you were on God's side, he was your friend. But if not, you were his mortal enemy, fit only for slaughter. It was an *attitude* desperately in search of Christians today!

Numbers 23:21 tells us the shout of a king is *among them*. A man among men is the one who fearlessly shouts out the truth because he knows who he is in Christ. Jesus is King of kings and Lord of lords (Revelation 17:14;19:16). The Radical Remnant are the kings and lords Jesus is King and Lord over. As such, men among them know their shout of victory is the death knell for any of God's enemies. While other believers act like whipped dogs under the boot of evil men and their ungodly decrees, men among them rise up and shout for joy, because they know God takes pleasure in the prosperity of those who favor His righteous cause (Psalms 35:27). Men among them are blessed by God for a purpose—to fearlessly and aggressively fund worldwide evangelism.

> *Phinehas the son of Eleazar, the son of Aaron the priest, has turned back My wrath from the children of Israel, **because he was zealous with My zeal among them,** so that I did not consume the children of Israel in My zeal.*

> —NUMBERS 25:11

The Radical Remnant is the army within the army, men among them who stand in the gap to literally save nations from catastrophic judgment. They are the ones who are zealous with God's zeal. Would that be you today?

PART TWO:

THE SOLUTION

CHAPTER SIX

Separation Is Mandatory

*"Therefore, **come out from among them and be separate,"** says the Lord. "Do not touch what is unclean, and I will receive you."*

—2 Corinthians 6:17

In December of each year, I spend time in prayer, asking the Lord for an MKMI ministry "theme" for the coming year. In the Philippines, we have hundreds of churches, pastors, Bible school students, and Christian workers that look to me as their father-in-faith. Therefore, I want to provide them with a God-given theme that all of us can rally around, so we're all in sync as an organization, striving together for the interests of the kingdom of God.

Sometimes God has given me a verse to stand on. Other times He has given me a word, phrase, or sentence based upon a Bible truth. When seeking the Lord in December 2019 for the year 2020, He gave me one word: *separation*. Of course, He knew what was coming even though we didn't. Without question, 2020 was the most challenging year of our lives, and I don't think anyone could dispute that truth. COVID-19 has run amok across the earth, spreading its tentacles of fear and evil influence into every level of society, and will continue to do so well into our foreseeable future. Many have died physically, and many more have been infected with this virus from hell. But the biggest tragedy is the fear cloud it has draped over planet Earth. Multitudes worldwide now live with not just a mask of fear over their face, but also a mask of fear over their lives.

It's exactly what Jesus prophesied in Luke 21:25-26—men's hearts failing them from fear of what they see coming on the earth. Yes indeed, the signs of our Lord's return are everywhere if one has eyes to see them. Whether He comes at this time or years from now, we need to stay *rapture ready*. Part of that readiness requires daily separation to the Lord.

When God gave me that theme word for 2020, initially I thought He was talking to me personally. With the end-times in mind, I thought He was emphasizing the need to stay as sharp as I could be individually, leaving no openings for the flesh or the devil in my life. This is how I planned to move into 2020. I made it my goal, and communicated that goal to all of our churches and personnel under the MKMI umbrella. My fatherly exhortation to them was the same as it was for me—to be more sanctified and separated to God than ever. But as the new year began to unfold the way it did, I realized that God's ministry theme word for us entailed much more than just our personal separation to Jesus. Through all that has happened, *I have come to understand that while individual separation is needed for the challenges of 2020 and beyond, so is separation from lukewarm Christians and wolves in sheep's clothing!* Why? For the work we are called to carry out as watchmen for the Lord.

Understand this one thing: the COVID-19 Fear Virus is a pandemic planned from hell itself. Satan is the author of this, not China. He simply used the Chinese as His delivery vehicle into the earth. The devil's one goal in mind was to create such a fear of death, it would cripple and paralyze worldwide efforts to carry out the Great Commission of Mark 16:15-18. This has been fulfilled exactly as he intended. In every corner of the globe we see quarantines, travel restrictions, lockdowns, businesses and schools shuttered, etc. *All of it was designed to stop the work of the church in reaching the lost.* How many people have contracted this Fear Virus and died without receiving Jesus as Savior? And how many more have died lost because the saints have been prevented from going to them with the gospel? Only God knows, but I guarantee it numbers into the millions.

And what about America in particular? Satan knew the USA was the most missions-minded nation in history, raised up by God to be the brightest light of gospel evangelism worldwide. He also knew there was a presidential election in November, and President Trump could not be reelected if he was to continue his plan to weaponize his Fear Virus and use it to shut down evangelism indefinitely. This is why there is undeniable proof that the election results were illegally tampered with and altered. There are many more sub-plots and side trails we could take regarding the plans and purposes for Satan launching this *PLANdemic*, but for the topic of this book, this is all we need to know. Total separation unto God is absolutely necessary now! Separation from sin and the unregenerate flesh. Separation from carnal and compromised Christians. Separation from wolves in sheep's clothing. As it says in James 2:12, everything we say and do must be done in light of the law of liberty, which is the law of love (1 John 3:23;4:21). That kind of liberty can only be realized when we become part of God's Radical Remnant.

> But in a great house there are not only vessels of gold and silver, but also of wood and clay, some for honor and some for dishonor. Therefore if anyone **cleanses himself from the latter,** he will be a vessel for honor, **sanctified and useful for the Master, prepared for every good work.** Flee also youthful lusts; but pursue righteousness, faith, love, peace with those who call on the Lord out of a pure heart.
>
> — 2 TIMOTHY 2:20-22

Our watchman responsibilities demand cleansing from the "latter." The Radical Remnant knows what Paul knew, and how important this was to him and to us now. Jesus said Paul *must suffer many things* for the name of Jesus (Acts 9:15), and most certainly he did. Read the book of 2 Corinthians, chapters 1, 4, 6, and 11. Paul presents a long list of things he suffered for the name of Jesus, exactly as Jesus said he would. So then, how did he hold his own all the way from start to finish, without carnal compromise (double-minded lifestyle), premature failure (quitting), or premature departure (early death)? The secret is found in his opening statement to the Roman church.

CHAPTER SEVEN

Keys to Longevity

*Paul, a **bondservant** of Jesus Christ, **called** to be an apostle, **separated** to the gospel of God.*

—ROMANS 1:1

P aul understood what we need to understand today. Notice the three parts to this opening verse to the Roman church. First, he called himself a bondservant of Jesus Christ. Second, he called himself an apostle. Third, he said he was separated to the gospel of God. In order to live the life of true separation as a member of the Radical Remnant, we must understand what it means to be God's bondservant, and to realize each one of us has a full-time calling in ministry as ambassadors of Christ (2 Corinthians 5:20).

New Testament writers frequently referred to themselves as bondservants of Jesus. We've already looked at how Paul addressed himself when writing his letter to the Roman believers, but he opened many of his other letters the same way. Here is how he greeted the Galatian churches: *"For do I now persuade men, or God? Or do I seek to please men? For if I still pleased men, I would not be a **bondservant of Christ**"* (Galatians 1:10).

He also greeted Titus in similar fashion in Titus 1:1. When Paul wrote to the Colossian church, he spoke of Epaphras, referring to him as a bondservant of Christ (Colossians 4:12). James, Peter, and Jude all did the same, opening their letters by identifying themselves as bondservants of Christ (James 1:1; 2 Peter 1:1; Jude 1:1).

Bondservants follow orders. They obey commands. Bondservants don't have the luxury of choosing which orders to follow or which commands to keep. In today's church, we've got multitudes of people who are born-again but haven't got the slightest clue about what it means to be a bondservant. To them, God doesn't give commands—He gives suggestions and requests. Disobedience to the clear commands in the Bible are everyday occurrences for the vast majority of people claiming to be children of God.

We love to talk about the benefits of being part of the Abrahamic Covenant in Christ, as described in Paul's letter to the Galatians (Galatians 3:15-29). It's truly a better covenant than the Old Covenant (Testament), based upon better promises (Hebrews 7:22; 8:6). But if you read the list of blessings attached to our covenant now, you'll find that all of those promised blessings are conditional. Go back and see it for yourself! God specifically ties the reception of His blessings to our *prior decision to keep His commandments* (Deuteronomy 28:1-14).

Our Lord Jesus set the perfect example for this, as described in the letter Paul wrote to the Philippians: *"Let this mind be in you which was also in Christ Jesus, who, being in the form of God, did not consider it robbery to be equal with God, but made Himself of no reputation, **taking the form of a bondservant,** and coming in the likeness of men,"* (Philippians 2:5-7).

Was our Lord ever tempted to disobey God, to try and convince His Heavenly Father there might be some other way to purchase our salvation? Yes. Was He ever emotionally upset, because as God's Bondservant, He knew He was required to follow orders to the letter? Yes. Did He ever yield to any of these temptations to sin through disobedience? No. Never. *Thank God!*

> *Who, in the days of His flesh, when He had offered up prayers and supplications, with **vehement** cries and tears to Him who was able to save Him from death, and was heard because of His godly fear, though He was a Son, yet He **learned obedience** by the things which He suffered.*
>
> —HEBREWS 5:7-8

> *He went a little farther and fell on His face, and prayed, saying, "O My Father, if it is possible, let this cup pass from Me; nevertheless, **not as I will, but as You will.**" Again, a second time, He went away and prayed, saying, "O My Father, if this cup cannot pass away from Me unless I drink it, **Your will be done.**"*
>
> —MATTHEW 26:39,42

The Bible says Jesus was tempted in all points like we are (Hebrews 4:15), yet He never sinned. Going one step further, the Lord was commanded to do things you and I will never be commanded to do, so not only was He tempted in every area we're tempted in, He faced *additional temptations* just because of Who He was, and what He came to earth to do (Hebrews 10:5-14).

When the time came to offer Himself up for our sins, His humanity recoiled at the prospect of what that meant. Crucifixion is still one of the most painful ways a person can be put to death, and the Romans perfected the art. It was a common method of torture and death for enemies of the Roman Empire, and Jesus knew this. He also knew that when He was made to be sin for us on that cross, He would suffer the agony of being forsaken by God (2 Corinthians 5:21; Mark 15:34). In prayer, sweating great drops of blood in the garden of Gethsemane, He pleaded with God to give Him an out—any other way to do what had to be done. He cried out in tears *vehemently.* That word is an adverb, and is defined as *a forceful, passionate, or intense manner; with great feeling.* That's how Jesus was praying to God. Forcefully. Passionately. Intensely with great emotion. For what? To *not do* what He was being told to do!

But Jesus knew He was God's Bondservant, so He went on and suffered through the physical horrors of the cross and the worst terror of all—3 days and 3 nights in hell as our sin-substitute. This is why He is now addressed as the First-Born from the dead (Revelation 1:5). The Son of God showed us the way. We must be like He was when He was here on earth. We're bondservants. We don't question God's commands. We don't ignore and disobey His orders. Jesus is now the Head of the Church, and the Commander of the army of the Lord, of which all Christians are a part. We do what He says, the way He says, when He says.

Each bondservant in Christ has a calling in this life. That calling includes certain commands that pertain to everybody in the army of the Lord. Some examples: we're all commanded to be holy as God is holy (1 Peter 1:15-16; 1 Thessalonians 4:3-7). We're all commanded to be strong (Joshua 1:9). We're all commanded to spread the gospel and make disciples (Mark 16:15-18; Matthew 28:18-20). But because no two people are alike, there are certain commands that apply to each of us individually, which don't apply to others. There is no such thing as a Christian with no specific, personal assignment from God. I use myself as an example. Because I'm called into the office of apostle, my responsibilities will differ from prophets, evangelists, pastors, and teachers. In fact, the apostolic office has elements of all five of these ministry gifts in operation, but the way I'm hard-wired by God will be different than how, let's say, a pastor would be. My apostolic calling is also restricted to certain countries, not all countries, as it was with Paul (1 Corinthians 9:2). One office isn't any better than any other, just different. That's why we need all five of these ministry gifts in the last days.

But even if believers are not called by God into full-time pulpit ministry like an apostle, prophet, evangelist, pastor, or teacher, we are all called as full-time ambassadors for Christ (Ephesians 6:20). That means every Christian has the responsibility to represent Jesus wherever they are, 24/7. That's the calling every child of God has, and the gifts and callings of God are without repentance (Romans 11:29). So, recognize your calling! When you got saved, you became a citizen of heaven (Philippians 3:20), got drafted into God's army and were made an official ambassador to earth. As such, you might be called by God to have a business, be in politics, teach in schools, or work at thousands of other professions out there. But no matter what we do in a secular sense, we must never forget we are called to be full-time representatives of heaven, fulfilling every command we get from God, as ordered. They're not suggestions or requests. They're commands and orders direct from "the top." Bondservant . . . you must carry out your orders and fulfill your calling—collectively and individually.

When we understand we're bondservants with both a collective and individual calling in life, we realize the absolute necessity for total separation to the gospel of God. There can be no tolerance for lukewarm, double-minded, half-hearted Christianity in our lives. This is how Paul was able to stay committed, dedicated, and faithful to God's call on his life. Near the end of his life, he wrote letters to instruct and encourage certain sons in the faith. He told Timothy the time of his "departure" was at hand. This is how he described the life he had lived: *"I have fought the good fight, I have finished the race, I have kept the faith"* (2 Timothy 4:7).

There is such a note of victory in this statement! He fought, finished, and kept whatever God entrusted to him. He was leaving earth on God's terms, not the devil's. Nobody can suffer like he did, and reach the end of life like this, without understanding the importance of being God's bondservant, called into ministry and separated to the gospel of God. These are the soldiers of the cross who make up the Radical Remnant. They don't quit, retreat, or surrender. They are constantly moving forward in the name of Jesus, advancing under enemy fire. What God told Moses in Exodus 14:15 is what the Lord Jesus tells us today. *Go forward!* Stop complaining and whining about all of your problems! God expects us to make the decision to become members of the Radical Remnant. When we do, we'll stop murmuring about the difficulties we face, and get busy moving forward into the lost, dark world in which we live.

CHAPTER EIGHT

Separated to Whom?

*"Now separate **to Me** Barnabas and Saul
for the work to which I have called them."*

—Acts 13:2

The Radical Remnant is a separated unit
within the Body of Christ. They understand
they work for the Holy Spirit, no one else. They
might be part of some organization or denom-
ination, but they're allegiance is to the Third
Person of the Trinity. If ever there is conflict
between what the Holy Spirit wants them to do,
and what some man-made group wants them to
do, they say "goodbye" to the works of men, and
go on with God 100 percent. Paul spoke about
this emphatically to the Galatian churches:

*For do I now persuade men, or God? Or do
I seek to please men?* **For if I still pleased
men, I would not be a bondservant of Christ.**

—GALATIANS 1:10

Paul declared his complete allegiance to
God, no matter who liked it or not. He knew
He was a bondservant *and* a radical follower of
Jesus Christ. We must make the same declaration. Psalms 118:8-9 declares it's better to put
our trust in God rather than in men. To place all
our trust in God means we follow the Holy Spirit
explicitly. We may "submit" to higher authorities
in a secular organization or environment somewhere, but that loyalty is *always* second-fiddle
to the plans, purposes, and timetables set by the
Spirit of God.

When the Antioch church was busy fasting,
praying, and waiting on the Lord, the Holy Spirit
spoke. When He did, He told the brethren to
separate certain men *to Him*, and no other. That's
a great question each of us must settle from the
start. To whom will we ultimately answer to?
The Radical Remnant knows it won't be anyone
on earth. They know they'll one day stand at

the judgment seat of Christ, to answer for the decisions they've made in life. They know the opinions of men won't matter then, so they don't matter now.

Like Paul, we must choose this mindset and lifestyle. Years ago, before I went to the Philippines for the first time, I came across a small desktop paper weight in the Oral Roberts University gift shop. I bought it and still have it. It reads: *To avoid criticism, say nothing, do nothing, be nothing*. Those are good words to remember. When we separate to the Holy Spirit, we understand He is the One Who gives us our marching orders, and He is the One Who we answer to—no other.

If we want our lives to amount to nothing of spiritual significance for God, then we must choose to paralyze ourselves through fear of criticism. If we do all we can to please the devil and those who do his bidding, our lives become nothing more than exhibits of wasted potential and opportunity. History is full of examples of saints who chose persecution, torment, torture, and even martyrdom, all because they refused to quit following the Holy Spirit. Today, all over the world, multitudes of believers suffer terribly for the faith which was once for all delivered to us by the Holy Spirit (Jude 1:3). They refuse to compromise because they made that choice at the same time they chose to receive Jesus as Lord and Savior. Just like Jesus in 1 John 3:16, the Radical Remnant is prepared to obey God all the way as well, no matter where we live, even if it means our death. Without hesitation or apology, we are separated to the Holy Spirit, which means we are separated to the gospel.

CHAPTER NINE

Separated to What?

*Paul, a bondservant of Jesus Christ, called to be an apostle, **separated to the gospel of God.***

—ROMANS 1:1

Because the Radical Remnant is separated to the Holy Spirit, they're also separated to the gospel of God. They aren't a bunch of limp noodles, masquerading as Christian soldiers. No sir! They follow God fearlessly. They're bold the way they should be (Ephesians 6:19-20), and that's it. They're not striving to be "Pastor Popular" or "Brother Blend-in." They don't water down the Bible. They don't alter obvious declarations about what God calls sin. They don't cherry-pick verses, observing only the ones that fit their lifestyle of compromise and perversion. They don't try to please a bunch of lukewarm hypocrites who claim to follow Christ. They don't care how they're received or rejected by the world. They're not a bunch of barely-born-again "stealth Christians," doing their best to camouflage their relationship with Jesus because they're afraid of offending the ungodly. No sir! Paul encountered people like this in the Corinthian church. As a member of God's Radical Remnant, here is how he responded and put them in their place when they tried to muzzle his ministry:

> *But with me it is a very small thing that I should be judged by you or by a human court. In fact, I do not even judge myself.*

> — 1 CORINTHIANS 4:3

Paul delivered the unadulterated gospel—the good, the bad, and the ugly, as written. He didn't care who was offended by it, and neither should we be. Later in the same letter, he told his disciples to imitate him as he imitated Christ (1 Corinthians 11:1). That's good advice. Go back and review the interaction Jesus had with His critics and religious hypocrites. Here's one example:

*"Why do you not understand My speech? Because you are not able to listen to My word. **You are of your father the devil, and the desires of your father you want to do.** He was a murderer from the beginning, and does not stand in the truth, because there is no truth in him. When he speaks a lie, he speaks from his own resources, for he is a liar and the father of it. Yet you have not known Him, but I know Him. And if I say, 'I do not know Him,' **I shall be a liar like you;** but I do know Him and keep His word."*

—JOHN 8:43-44,55

Does this exchange lead you to believe Jesus was campaigning for votes because He was planning to run for Jerusalem City Council in upcoming elections? Hardly! Paul exhorted his disciples to follow him as he followed Christ. This kind of in-your-face boldness is the result! The Radical Remnant knows Who to follow, and Who to imitate. It becomes the bedrock for the work we must complete in Jesus' name.

CHAPTER TEN

Separated for What?

"Now separate to Me Barnabas and Saul
***for the work** to which I have called them."*

—Acts 13:2

When we make the decision to join the ranks of the Radical Remnant, we must understand what this will mean for the rest of our lives, and how it will change the desires of our heart. Paul had four main desires he set forth as benchmarks for doctrinal accuracy and ministry longevity. They are listed in his letter to the Philippians:

*That I may know Him and the power of His resurrection, and **the fellowship of His suffering,** being conformed to His death.*

—Philippians 3:10

How many sermons do we here today about desiring these four things because we're Christian? Not very many! To know Jesus. To know the power of His resurrection. To fellowship with His sufferings. To be conformed to His death. These four desires are top priority for members of God's Radical Remnant, as they were for Paul. Volumes could be written about each of the four, but for the purposes of this book, let's isolate number three.

Paul *wanted* to fellowship with the sufferings that Jesus suffered. This is not talking about the crucifixion. That was a substitutionary work Jesus did *for us*. The fellowship of our Lord's sufferings will separate the men from among them, because it deals with the ongoing work of ministry in the name of Jesus. It's preaching a righteous message in an unrighteous world. It's presenting the light of the gospel, while having to contend with all the hatred, animosity, and resistance stirred up by those who love living in the dark (John 3:19-21).

In the end times, Christians must prepare for the dramatic increase in persecution coming our way—especially in nations that haven't experienced it that much, such as the USA. Yes, Jesus said we are to take His yoke, relax, and learn from Him (Matthew 11:28). But that doesn't mean we will just cruise through life on a magic carpet of prosperity and happiness. In the midst of testing and trials, we need to stay steadfast and determined to stand our ground for the truth.

> **Blessed are you** when men hate you, and when they exclude you, and revile you, and cast out your name as evil, for the Son of Man's sake. **Rejoice in that day and leap for joy!** For indeed your reward is great in heaven, for in like manner their fathers did to the prophets.
>
> — LUKE 6:22-23

More and more, we're going to be tempted to compromise our message under pressure, just like Shadrach, Meshach, and Abednego in Daniel 3:16-18, and Daniel himself in Daniel 6:6-10. Members of the Radical Remnant will never yield to any threat seeking to turn them away from their ministry assignments. And remember, *every* Christian has a ministry assignment. God has a plan for each and every one of us. How we respond is up to us, not up to God.

CHAPTER ELEVEN

Two Out of Twelve

*Except for **Caleb** the son of Jephunneh and **Joshua** the son of Nun, you shall by no means enter the land which I swore I would make you dwell in.*

—NUMBERS 14:30

Study Numbers chapters 13 and 14. Moses was instructed by God to pick one person from each of the twelve tribes to go spy out the Promised Land to see who and what was over there. They were all seasoned, experienced leaders. They weren't a bunch of newbies. After forty days, they came back to give their intelligence report to Moses and the nation. This was God's ministry assignment for them at that time.

When it was all over, the Jews had successfully talked themselves right out of God's blessings, favor, protection, and provision. Why? Because they did what so many Christians do today—they believed the majority report. Ten out of the twelve spies gave an evil report of unbelief (Numbers 14:37). It wasn't just a bad report . . . God called it an *evil* report. When confronted with opposing viewpoints of faith verses fear, the majority report ruled the day. Choosing to believe the ten rather than the two, all the people lifted up their voices with tears and remorse, accepting defeat by default. The more Joshua and Caleb tried to convince them to trust God, the more the faithless mob looked for stones to stone them.

What was the real difference between the two and the ten? The ten giving the evil report of fear chose to only see how big their enemies were. The two giving the good report of faith chose to only see how big their God was. They knew they had a covenant with God and the ungodly squatters across the river didn't. The difference was in what these twelve spies chose to look at.

There were twelve men selected to spy out the land, and their names are listed in Numbers 13:4-15. That's the last you ever hear of the unbelieving ten. On the other hand, the two who gave the good report of faith become key figures in the Bible from then until now. To this day, Joshua and Caleb are studied, looked up to, and imitated by the modern-day Radical Remnant. These two understood the importance of separating themselves from the majority who cower and cave in to fear. As it was then, so it is today. The Radical Remnant refuses to give God evil reports of doubt and unbelief, no matter how impossible situations may look in the natural.

I've traveled in full-time ministry since 1980, fellowshipping with multitudes of believers of different nations, cultures, and languages. Without hesitation, I will say the percentage of people who make up today's Radical Remnant is about the same as what we see here thousands of years ago at the banks of the Jordan River. Like Caleb, the Radical Remnant is comprised of children of God who *have a different spirit* about them. In today's world, for every twelve New Testament believers, ten are worthless to God for the work of ministry. Only two are "meet" for the Master's use (2 Timothy 2:21).

CHAPTER TWELVE

Whose Friend Are You?

*Adulterers and adulteresses! Do you not know that **friendship with the world is enmity with God?** Whoever therefore wants to be a friend of the world **makes himself** an enemy of God.*

—JAMES 4:4

*And the Scripture was fulfilled which says, "Abraham believed God, and it was accounted to him for righteousness." **And he was called the friend of God.***

—JAMES 2:23

Not all Christians are members of God's Radical Remnant because not all Christians are friends of God. These two verses identify the two groups within the church today. God loves all of His children equally, but when it comes to *doing meaningful things* for the Lord, one group is useful and the other one isn't. Both groups are comprised of saved people on their way to heaven, but the friendships they have on earth is another matter entirely.

Believers are either friends of God or friends of the world, in the same way believers are part of God's Radical Remnant, or not. As far as God is concerned, when it comes to the issue of friendship, it's one or the other. Those are the only two options available to us. If Christians don't make themselves friends of God, they make themselves friends with the world, which by default makes them enemies of God.

Sadly, these are the believers who get pulled back into the old sinful lifestyle they were set free from, or the believers who never really got free from their flesh in the first place. Of course, God wants all His children to be friends with Him because He wants every Christian to be radical for the cause of Christ—completely separated in spirit, soul, and body (1 Thessalonians 5:23). But that is not the case most of the time. It's very easy for believers to choose friendship with the world and enmity with God—that's why their group represents the vast majority of born-again people. When we let our dead-to-sin flesh rule and reign in our lives, we simultaneously forsake our responsibilities and ministry calling. It takes much more discipline and dedication to be called a friend of God. That's why the Radical Remnant is just that—a remnant.

Forsaking our ministry responsibilities and falling out of friendship with God is a distinct possibility, so beware. In 2 Peter 2:15, Peter compares Balaam's downfall to certain ones that he used to have meaningful fellowship with in ministry, who later on chose to forsake the right way. He called them dogs who eat their own vomit, and clean pigs who can't resist jumping back into the mud (2 Peter 2:22). The warning is obvious. People can't forsake the right way unless they've already been in the right way. This is exactly what Jesus warned us about in Luke 9:62, when He said we're not fit for the kingdom of God if we *look back* after putting our hand to the plow. Stay radical for Jesus. Protect your friendship with God.

In Luke 16:13, Jesus said we can't serve God and mammon, which represents the love of money (1 Timothy 6:10). We have to decide which master we will serve—it can't be both. Paul wrote to the Philippians, identifying certain staff members who had fallen away and gone back into the world, driven by selfishness and greed (Philippians 2:21). In the book of Hebrews, the writer (whom I believe was Paul), used Esau as the example of what not to do in ministry: exchange your heavenly rewards for temporal earthly pleasures (Hebrews 12:16-17). In John's first epistle, he warned his disciples not to love the world or the things in the world, because all of it is passing away (1 John 2:15-17). Peter also cautioned for the need to be spiritually vigilant—because if believers aren't careful, they can quickly forget what a filthy, sinful, and lost condition they were set free from (2 Peter 1:9). We have to decide once and for all whose friend we're going to be, and protect our friendship with God at all costs.

Paul had a disciple named Demas, who became the New Testament poster child for what not to do if you plan to victoriously reach the finish line of life in Christ. According to Colossians 4:14 and Philemon 1:24, once upon a time he was a trusted staff member in

Paul's ministry. But somewhere along the way, Demas started to look back. He started to drift from the right way. He forgot that it was not all about him, but about him serving others in the name of Jesus (Philippians 2:3-4). In short, all of the references we just reviewed were demonstrated in the life of Demas. When he realized he couldn't serve Jesus and the world at the same time, he forsook his ministry responsibilities and fell back into the world. Here's how Paul broke the news to Timothy:

> *Be diligent to come to me quickly; for Demas has forsaken me, having loved this present world, and has departed for Thessalonica.*

> —2 Timothy 4:9-10

Tragic, but unfortunately, very common. How do we make ourselves an enemy of God? Follow Demas. On the other hand, how do we make ourselves a friend of God, and maintain inclusion in God's Radical Remnant? Follow Abraham. *Sanctify and separate completely to God in faith – trusting God to do the impossible* (Romans 4:17-21). The choices Abraham made qualified him for friendship with God. They also moved him, and others like him, into the rarified air that only the Radical Remnant occupies. Jesus taught it like this:

> *"For there are eunuchs who were born thus from their mother's womb, and there are eunuchs who were made eunuchs by men, and **there are eunuchs who have made themselves eunuchs for the kingdom of heaven's sake. He who is able to accept it, let him accept it."***
>
> —MATTHEW 19:12

When the Lord talks about making oneself a eunuch for the kingdom of heaven's sake, He is talking about following His example. On earth, Jesus was totally separated from the world—living in it but not being of it (John 17:14-19). Notice He said this isn't easy . . . not everyone is determined enough to accept this challenge and rise to this level of sanctification. Most believers can't make the cut because they're too much in love with the temporal things of this world. That's why Matthew 22:14 tells us many are called *but few are chosen*.

Eunuchs who make themselves eunuchs for the Lord's sake make themselves friends of God, and make themselves members of the Radical Remnant simultaneously. Every believer is called to excellence in the last days. There are no excuses for lethargy, laziness, apathy, or fear. None of this is haphazard or accidental. It is a pre-meditated, calculated journey from faith to faith (Romans 1:17). Eunuchs for the kingdom of heaven make themselves who they are by the way they live their life. Yes, without God's grace we couldn't do anything, but because He gave it we can utilize the greatest weapon available to us—free will (1 Corinthians 15:10; Joshua 24:15). Once again, the Bible provides key guidelines for measuring our qualifications.

Keep your heart with all diligence, for out of it spring the issues of life. Put away from you a deceitful mouth, and put perverse lips far from you. Let your eyes look straight ahead, and your eyelids look right before you. Ponder the path of your feet, and let all your ways be established. Do not turn to the right or the left; remove your foot from evil.

—PROVERBS 4:23-27

When we diligently monitor the three areas listed here, we make ourselves friends with God and members of His Radical Remnant. First, the tongue. Joshua 1:8 tells us to keep God's Word in our mouth at all times. We are to meditate in it day and night so we can follow His commandments explicitly. Then we will become prosperous and successful in life. James 3:1-2 says that if we control our tongue, we control our whole body. Proverbs 18:21 says death and life are in the power of the tongue. Next, the eyes. Colossians 3:1-2 tells us to set our eyes on things above, so we can see that the reality of this world is always subject to the reality in the unseen world (2 Corinthians 4:18; 2 Kings 6:15-18). Finally, the feet. When we ponder the path of our feet, we're charting the direction of our life. This comes about by renewing our minds to the Word of God (Romans 12:1-3), so we're moving in sync with the Holy Spirit. Like Jesus, we're then in position to be used in the realm of the miraculous, walking with God's stamp of approval (Acts 2:22).

CHAPTER THIRTEEN

The Choice Is Yours

Then one of the seraphim flew to me, having in his hand a live coal which he had taken with the tongs from the altar. And he touched my mouth with it, and said: "Behold, this has touched your lips; your iniquity is taken away, and your sin purged." Also I heard the voice of the Lord saying: "Whom shall I send, and who will go for Us?" **Then I said, "Here am I! Send me."**

—ISAIAH 6:6-8

In all my years of serving Jesus, this question in Isaiah 6:6-8 never ceases to amaze me. I still shake my head in awe and wonder! What a great honor, and what a great responsibility! Proverbs 24:11-12 says it best:

Deliver those who are drawn toward death, and hold back those stumbling to the slaughter. If you say, "Surely we did not know this," does not He who weighs the hearts consider it? He who keeps your soul, does He not know it? **And will He not render to each man according to his deeds?**

"Operation Separation" begins with us. Only then can we move on to the separation from carnal Christians and wolves in sheep's clothing. We can't effectively separate from the last two until we separate from our own carnal appetites. Our iniquities and sins need to be purged to be a part of this army within the army.

> *"Or how can you say to your brother, 'Let me remove the speck from your eye'; and look, a plank is in your own eye? Hypocrite!* ***First remove the plank from your own eye,*** *and then you will see clearly to remove the speck from your brother's eye."*
>
> —MATTHEW 7:4-5

Holiness, purity, and righteous living *never* go out of style. Paul bluntly told the Corinthians he could end up as a castaway from the anointing of God if he didn't keep his body under control (1 Corinthians 9:27). So then, *keep your body under control!* Nobody can do that for you except you.

Personal separation precedes the decision to separate from lukewarm, carnal Christians. We don't stop loving them, we just choose to love them from a distance. The Bible says a little leaven leavens the whole lump (1 Corinthians 5:6; Galatians 5:7-9). Many other verses say the same thing. We should freely fellowship with *any* believer because we're commanded to love *one another* as Jesus loves us (John 13:34-35). But remember, the Lord had seventy part-time disciples and twelve full-time disciples, with three of those twelve making up His "inner circle." He didn't relate to everyone the same way, and neither should we.

Finally, the Radical Remnant is constantly on alert for wolves in sheep's clothing (2 Corinthians 11:12-15). They are everywhere in this day and age, sent by Satan to infiltrate the Body of Christ (Philippians 3:2; Colossians 2:8; 2 Peter 3:17). They will deceive many in the last days (Matthew 24:3-5), so beware. Only God can judge a person's heart (1 Samuel 16:7), but we are commanded to judge their doctrines and lifestyle, according to the Word of God. Don't follow or yield to them. Give them no place in your life, and warn others as often as necessary (Galatians 2:5).

Make your choice now. Don't wait. If you're part of God's Radical Remnant, good for you. If you're moving in the right direction, good for you. Surround yourself with stronger soldiers than you, and make them your best friends. If you're just starting this journey, congratulations! You've made the wisest decision any Christian can make. If you've been sleeping at your post, it's time to wake up and get in the game! God is asking you now: *Will you go for Me? Can I depend upon you?* I replied like Isaiah a long time ago. Trust me—if you do the same, it will pay rich dividends in this life and the next. There's a place for you in God's Radical Remnant. Time is short. We need you now!

ABOUT THE AUTHOR

Mike Keyes grew up in Ohio and was raised in the Roman Catholic church. In 1973, he graduated from college to become a successful advertising executive and graphic artist. On September 21, 1978, at age twenty-six, he was born again and Spirit filled two days later. Immediately, the gifts of the Spirit began working in his life. Through his local church, he began to witness on the streets, in area prisons, and anywhere he could hand out tracts.

In September 1979, Reverend Keyes resigned his job to attend Rhema Bible Training Center in Tulsa, Oklahoma, graduating in May 1980. In September 1980, he traveled to the Philippines with a oneway plane ticket, arriving without knowledge of the language or customs and with no one there to meet him. When he got off that plane to begin his ministry, he had twenty dollars in his pocket, one footlocker containing his Bible, class notes, a few changes of clothing, and the promise of support totaling $250 from no one except his parents and one small church in Toledo, Ohio.

From those humble beginnings and through his faithfulness to the calling of God over the years, the Lord has used Reverend Keyes extensively to reach untold numbers of people in the Philippines and around the world. Always emphasizing outreach to the remote, overlooked, out-of-the-way villages and towns that no one else has gone to, it is conservatively estimated that since the beginning of his ministry's outreach in 1980, over 750,000 souls have been won to Christ in his nationwide crusades in the Philippines.

Mike Keyes Ministries International (MKMI) is an apostolic ministry that reaches the lost, teaches the Christians, and trains the ministers. With a consistent crusade outreach, a church network of hundreds of churches, and the Rhema Bible Training Center, Reverend Keyes and his staff, pastors, graduates, and students continue to fulfill the Great Commission wherever he is instructed to go by the Holy Spirit—throughout the Philippines and around the world.

Reverend Keyes is married to a native Filipina, Ethel, and has two children.

OTHER BOOKS BY THE AUTHOR

Advancing Under Fire
Be Strong, Stay Strong
Divine Peace
Hope
Military Mentality
The Language of Faith
You Can Be Who You Already Are
Determined Faith

www.mkmi.org
www.mkmi.info